MINIMS

or, Man Is The Only Animal That Wears Bow Ties.

Written and Illustrated by
TOM WELLER

HOUGHTON MIFFLIN COMPANY · BOSTON · 1982

TO DLG

Library of Congress Cataloging in Publication Data

Weller, Tom.
Minims, or, Man is the only animal that wears bow ties.
1. Epigrams, American. I. Title. II. Title: Man is
the only animal that wears bow ties.
PN6281.W37 1982   818'.5402   82-11724
ISBN 0-395-32938-8 (pbk.)

Printed in the United States of America

D 10 9 8 7 6 5 4 3 2 1

minim (min′ əm) *n:* a statement expressed in proverbial or sentential form but having no general application or practical use whatever—compare MAXIM.

Two heads are more numerous than one.

An empty bus travels fast.

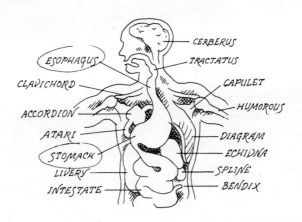

CERBERUS

ESOPHAGUS

TRACTATUS

CLAVICHORD

CAPULET

ACCORDION

HUMOROUS

ATARI

DIAGRAM

STOMACH

ECHIDNA

LIVERY

SPLINE

INTESTATE

BENDIX

The way to a man's stomach
is through his esophagus.

A watched clock never boils.

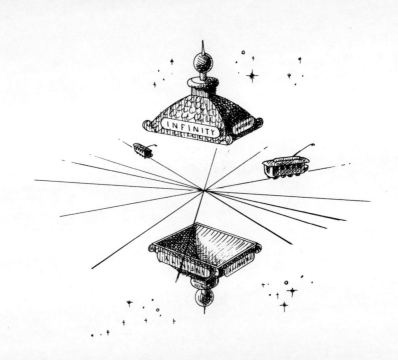

Infinity is where you transfer
from one parallel line to another.

Live and lean.

The bigger they are, the harder they hit.

A burning dog needs no chimney.

The more things change, the more they stay insane.

Scissors always travel in pairs.

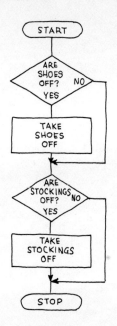

You have to take off your shoes
before you can take off your stockings.

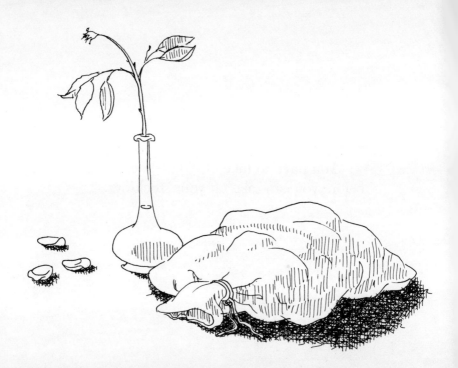

A bed of roses is not at all the same
as a sack of frogs.

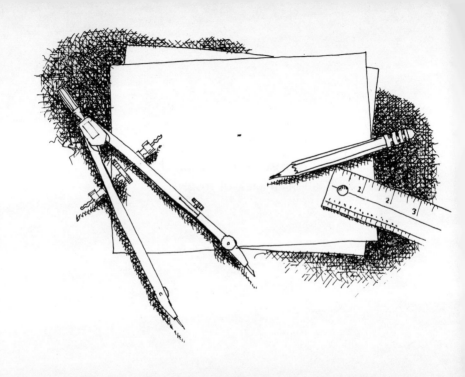

A straight line is the shortest distance between one point.

You can fool all of the people some of the time; you can fool some of the people all of the time; and that should be sufficient for most purposes.

Money is its own reward.

Long journeys seldom begin in Chinese restaurants.

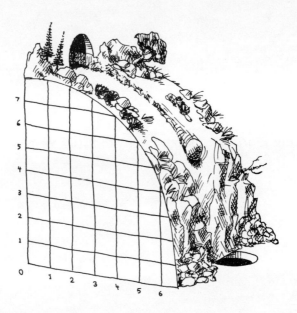

A rolling stone gathers momentum.

Just because something is pretty
doesn't mean it's good to eat.

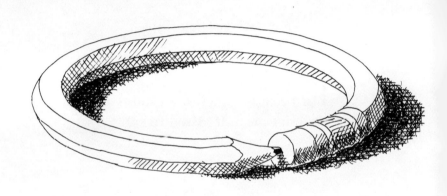

A pencil with no point needs no eraser.

Where there's smoke, there's pollution.

Pigs and goats alike care nothing for the opera.

A hatrack is not an amusing companion.

Rain before seven, dark before midnight.

Equality is the great leveler.

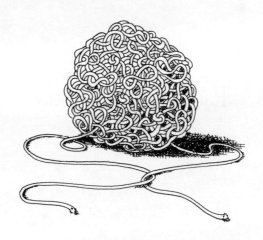

A piece of string has two ends but no beginning.

You'll catch more flies with honey than you care to.

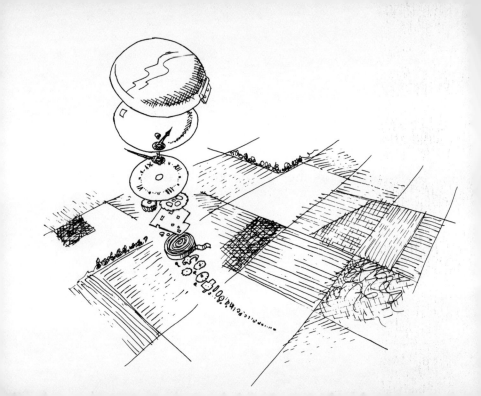

It is difficult to repair a watch while falling from an airplane.

The Lord loveth a wealthy giver.

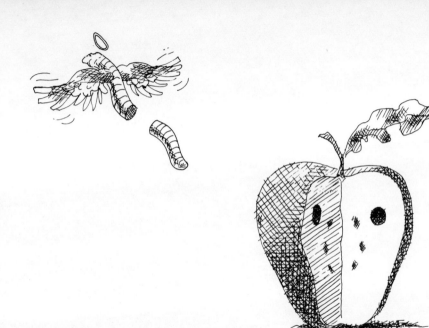

An apple a day makes 365 apples a year.

No one achieves immortality in his own lifetime.

The streetlight shines upon both
the just and the unjust.

ANNA POTATOES
12 FAST LANE
UPTOWN, HA 21212

No. 1212

May 12 19 99   12-1212
                1212

PAY TO THE
ORDER OF: *Flaky Bakery* ———————— $ 12 ××

A Dozen and no/1000 ——————————— **Dollars**

RIVER BANK
TREE BRANCH
ICEBURGH, HA 12121

Alma Potatoer

Memo ———————————————————

⊄:2121001:☺☐12···☐2112!

Twelve is as good as a dozen.

You'll get further with a kind word and a gun than with a kind word alone.

Time heals all non-fatal wounds.

Give me a lever long enough and a place to stand, and I will break my lever.

The hand is quicker than the foot.

Today is the first day of the rest of your week.

A drowned cat shuns the water.

Where there's a will, there's a won't.

The oyster is silent from necessity.

It is better to remain childless
than to father an orphan.

The early worm gets eaten by a bird.

Almost any misfortune is preferable to a worse one.

He who would achieve great things must first be born.

The road to hell is paved by the same contractors
as all the other roads.

A man with a cabbage for a head
will never want for nourishment.

You can't trust yourself over 30.

THIS MONTH

FRIDAY	FRIDAY	FRIDAY	FRIDAY	FRIDAY	FRIDAY	FRIDAY
		13	13	13 BAD FRIDAY	13	13
13	13 INCOME TAX DUE	13	13	13	13	13
13	13	13	13	13 GREAT FIRE OF LONDON, 1666	13	13
13	13	13	13	13	13	13 BLACK DEATH, 1347
13	13	13 JUDGEMENT DAY				

No month can have more than one Friday the 13th.   ʼ

Fortune favors the lucky.

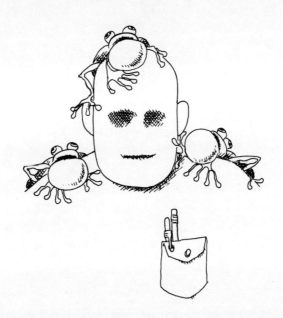

The croaking of frogs does not annoy the deaf.

Home is where the house is.

A knowledge of Sanskrit is of little use
to a man trapped in a sewer.

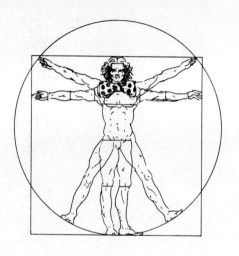

Man is the only animal that wears bow ties.

There are more things in heaven and earth than anyplace else.